2020 Catholic Planner

2020 Catholic Planner

The Month of the Holy Name of Jesus

JANUARY 2020

Sun.	Mon.	Tues.	Wed.	Thurs.	Fri.	Sat.
			1	2	3	4
5	6	7	8	9	10	11
12	13	14	15	16	17	18
19	20	21	22	23	24	25
26	27	28	29	30	31	

December 29, 2019-January 4, 2020

To-Do List:

_____   _____

_____   _____

_____   _____

_____   _____

_____   _____

_____   _____

I am praying for…

_____

_____

_____

I am thankful for…

_____

_____

_____

"Cheerfulness prepares a glorious mind
for all the noblest acts."
Saint Elizabeth Ann Seton

Sunday, December 29, 2019
The Holy Family of Jesus, Mary, and Joseph

Monday, December 30, 2019

Tuesday, December 31, 2019

Wednesday, January 1
Solemnity of Mary, the Holy Mother of God (Holy Day of Obligation)

Thursday, January 2

Friday, January 3
First Friday, The Most Holy Name of Jesus

Saturday, January 4
First Saturday, St. Elizabeth Ann Seton

January 5-11, 2020

To-Do List:

_____   _____

_____   _____

_____   _____

_____   _____

_____   _____

_____   _____

I am praying for…

_____

_____

_____

I am thankful for…

_____

_____

_____

"It is with the smallest brushes that the Artist paints the best paintings." – St. André Bessette

Sunday, January 5
The Epiphany of the Lord

Monday, January 6
St. André Bessette

Tuesday, January 7

Wednesday, January 8

Thursday, January 9

Friday, January 10

Saturday, January 11

January 12-18, 2020

To-Do List:

_____   _____

_____   _____

_____   _____

_____   _____

_____   _____

_____   _____

I am praying for…

_____

_____

_____

I am thankful for…

_____

_____

_____

"The saints did not all begin well, but they ended well."

St. John Vianney

Sunday, January 12
The Baptism of the Lord

Monday, January 13
St. Hilary

Tuesday, January 14

Wednesday, January 15

Thursday, January 16

Friday, January 17

Saturday, January 18

January 19-25, 2020

To-Do List:

_____   _____

_____   _____

_____   _____

_____   _____

_____   _____

_____   _____

I am praying for…

_____

_____

_____

I am thankful for…

_____

_____

_____

"God commands you to pray, but He forbids you to worry."
St. Francis de Sales

Sunday, January 19

Monday, January 20
Dr. Martin Luther King Jr. Day

Tuesday, January 21

Wednesday, January 22
Day of Prayer for the Legal Protection of Unborn Children

Thursday, January 23
St. Marianne Cope

Friday, January 24
St. Francis de Sales

Saturday, January 25
The Conversion of St. Paul

The Month of
the Passion of the
Lord

FEBRUARY 2020

Sun.	Mon.	Tues.	Wed.	Thurs.	Fri.	Sat.
						1
2	3	4	5	6	7	8
9	10	11	12	13	14	15
16	17	18	19	20	21	22
23	24	25	26	27	28	29

January 26 – February 1, 2020

To-Do List:

_____   _____

_____   _____

_____   _____

_____   _____

_____   _____

_____   _____

I am praying for…

_____

_____

_____

I am thankful for…

_____

_____

_____

"Do not try to excuse your faults; try to correct them."
St. John Bosco

Sunday, January 26

Monday, January 27

Tuesday, January 28
St. Thomas Aquinas

Wednesday, January 29

Thursday, January 30

Friday, January 31
St. John Bosco

Saturday, February 1
First Saturday

February 2-8, 2020

To-Do List:

check with Lourdes
for lunch on Dues.

Put debit Card
in handbag
watch EWTN 11:30

_____
_____
_____
_____
_____
_____

I am praying for…
Juniors increase
of membership -
Fr. David -

I am thankful for…
good health -

"It is not hard to obey when we love the one whom we obey."
St. Ignatius of Loyola

Sunday, February 2
The Presentation of the Lord

Monday, February 3
St. Blaise

Start Novena to O L of Lourdes

Tuesday, February 4

Lunch with Lourdes & John 12:45-

Wednesday, February 5
St. Agatha

Fr. David's birthday!
Go to schools for JRS -

Thursday, February 6
St. Paul Miki and Companions

Mass at 8:00 with Nida & Brunch
in hall - upcoming membership -
10:00

Friday, February 7
First Friday

Walmart -

Saturday, February 8
St. Josephine Bakhita

JRS -

February 9-15, 2020

To-Do List:

_____   _____

_____   _____

_____   _____

_____   _____

_____   _____

_____   _____

I am praying for…

_____

_____

_____

I am thankful for…

_____

_____

_____

"Love overcomes, love delights, those who love the Sacred Heart rejoice." – St. Bernadette Soubirous

Sunday, February 9

Monday, February 10
St. Scholastica

Tuesday, February 11
Our Lady of Lourdes

Wednesday, February 12

Thursday, February 13

Friday, February 14
Sts. Cyril and Methodius, St. Valentine's Day

Saturday, February 15

February 16-22, 2020

To-Do List:

_____   _____

_____   _____

_____   _____

_____   _____

_____   _____

_____   _____

I am praying for…

_____

_____

_____

I am thankful for…

_____

_____

_____

"As the soul is the life of the body, so the Holy Spirit is the life of our souls." - St. Peter Damian

Sunday, February 16

Monday, February 17
Presidents' Day

Tuesday, February 18

Wednesday, February 19

Thursday, February 20

Friday, February 21
St. Peter Damian

Saturday, February 22
The Chair of St. Peter the Apostle

February 23-29, 2020

To-Do List:

_____   _____

_____   _____

_____   _____

_____   _____

_____   _____

_____   _____

I am praying for…

_____

_____

_____

I am thankful for…

_____

_____

_____

"All that we do without offering it to God is wasted."
St. John Vianney

Sunday, February 23

Monday, February 24

Tuesday, February 25

Wednesday, February 26
Ash Wednesday (Day of Fasting and Abstinence)

Thursday, February 27

Friday, February 28

Saturday, February 29

The Month of St. Joseph

MARCH 2020

Sun.	Mon.	Tues.	Wed.	Thurs.	Fri.	Sat.
1	2	3	4	5	6	7
8	9	10	11	12	13	14
15	16	17	18	19	20	21
22	23	24	25	26	27	28
29	30	31				

March 1-7, 2020

To-Do List:

_____   _____

_____   _____

_____   _____

_____   _____

_____   _____

_____   _____

I am praying for…	I am thankful for…
_____	_____
_____	_____
_____	_____

"Never let your home be without a crucifix... that all who enter it may know that you are a disciple of a Crucified Lord." - Saint Jean Vianney

Sunday, March 1
First Sunday of Lent

Monday, March 2

Tuesday, March 3
St. Katharine Drexel

Wednesday, March 4

Thursday, March 5

Friday, March 6 ⤢
First Friday

Saturday, March 7
First Saturday, Sts. Perpetua and Felicity

March 8-14, 2020

To-Do List:

_____   _____

_____   _____

_____   _____

_____   _____

_____   _____

_____   _____

I am praying for…

_____

_____

_____

I am thankful for…

_____

_____

_____

"Whenever anything disagreeable or displeasing happens to you, remember Christ crucified and be silent."
Saint John of the Cross

Sunday, March 8
Second Sunday of Lent

Monday, March 9
St. Frances of Rome

Tuesday, March 10

Wednesday, March 11

Thursday, March 12

Friday, March 13

Saturday, March 14

March 15-21, 2020

To-Do List:

_____   _____

_____   _____

_____   _____

_____   _____

_____   _____

_____   _____

I am praying for…	I am thankful for…

"Mount Calvary is the academy of love."
St. Francis de Sales

Sunday, March 15
Third Sunday of Lent

Monday, March 16

Tuesday, March 17
St. Patrick

Wednesday, March 18

Thursday, March 19
St. Joseph, Spouse of the Blessed Virgin Mary

Friday, March 20

Saturday, March 21

March 22–28, 2020

To-Do List:

_____   _____

_____   _____

_____   _____

_____   _____

_____   _____

_____   _____

I am praying for…

_____

_____

_____

I am thankful for…

_____

_____

_____

"The world's thy ship and not thy home."
Saint Thérèse of Lisieux

Sunday, March 22
Fourth Sunday of Lent

Monday, March 23

Tuesday, March 24

Wednesday, March 25
The Annunciation of the Lord

Thursday, March 26

Friday, March 27

Saturday, March 28

The Month of the Most Holy Eucharist

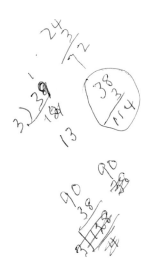

APRIL 2020

Sun.	Mon.	Tues.	Wed.	Thurs.	Fri.	Sat.
Call Ruby She owes me $38 for wreath for Faye — $90 flowers + 34 (service fees 3) 114 total			1	2	3	4
5	6	7 *38*	8	9	10	11
12	13	14	15	16	17	18
19	20	21	22	23	24	25
26	27	28	29	30		

March 29–April 4, 2020

To-Do List:

_____   _____

_____   _____

_____   _____

_____   _____

_____   _____

_____   _____

I am praying for…

_____

_____

_____

I am thankful for…

_____

_____

"While the world changes, the cross stands firm."
Saint Bruno

Sunday, March 29
Fifth Sunday of Lent

Monday, March 30

Tuesday, March 31

Wednesday, April 1

Thursday, April 2
St. Francis of Paola

Friday, April 3
First Friday, St. Richard of Chichester

Saturday, April 4
First Saturday, St. Isidore

April 5-11, 2020

To-Do List:

_____   _____

_____   _____

_____   _____

_____   _____

_____   _____

_____   _____

I am praying for…

_____

_____

_____

I am thankful for…

_____

_____

_____

"Apart from the cross, there is no other ladder by which we may get to heaven." - St. Rose of Lima

Sunday, April 5
Palm Sunday of the Passion of the Lord

Monday, April 6

Tuesday, April 7

Wednesday, April 8

Thursday, April 9
Holy Thursday

Friday, April 10 ✝
Good Friday (Day of Fasting and Abstinence)

Saturday, April 11
Holy Saturday

April 12-18, 2020

To-Do List:

_____   _____

_____   _____

_____   _____

_____   _____

_____   _____

_____   _____

I am praying for…

_____

_____

_____

I am thankful for…

_____

_____

_____

"We are the Easter people, and Alleluia is our song!"

St. John Paul II

Sunday, April 12
Easter Sunday of the Resurrection of the Lord

Monday, April 13

Tuesday, April 14

Wednesday, April 15

Thursday, April 16

Friday, April 17

Saturday, April 18

April 19-25, 2020

To-Do List:

———————————————   ———————————————

———————————————   ———————————————

———————————————   ———————————————

———————————————   ———————————————

———————————————   ———————————————

———————————————   ———————————————

I am praying for…

———————————————

———————————————

———————————————

I am thankful for…

———————————————

———————————————

———————————————

"I realize more and more how much every soul needs God's mercy throughout life and particularly at the hour of death."
St. Faustina

Sunday, April 19
Divine Mercy Sunday

Monday, April 20

Tuesday, April 21
St. Anselm

Wednesday, April 22

Thursday, April 23
St. George

Friday, April 24

Saturday, April 25
St. Mark, the Evangelist

The Month of
the Blessed Virgin
Mary

MAY 2020

Sun.	Mon.	Tues.	Wed.	Thurs.	Fri.	Sat.
					1	2
3	4	5	6	7	8	9
10	11	12	13	14	15	16
17	18	19	20	21	22	23
24	25	26	27	28	29	30
31						

April 26 – May 2, 2020

To-Do List:

_____   _____

_____   _____

_____   _____

_____   _____

_____   _____

_____   _____

I am praying for…

_____

_____

_____

I am thankful for…

_____

_____

_____

"If you are what you should be, you will set the whole world ablaze!" - Saint Catherine of Siena

Sunday, April 26

Monday, April 27

Tuesday, April 28
St. Louis de Montfort

Wednesday, April 29
St. Catherine of Siena

Thursday, April 30
Pope St. Pius V

Friday, May 1
First Friday, St. Joseph the Worker

Saturday, May 2
First Saturday, St. Athanasius

May 3-9, 2020

To-Do List:

_____   _____

_____   _____

_____   _____

_____   _____

_____   _____

_____   _____

I am praying for…

_____

_____

_____

I am thankful for…

_____

_____

_____

"The gate of heaven is very low; only the humble can enter it." - St. Elizabeth Ann Seton

Sunday, May 3

Monday, May 4

Tuesday, May 5

Wednesday, May 6

Thursday, May 7

Friday, May 8

Saturday, May 9

May 10-16, 2020

To-Do List:

_____   _____

_____   _____

_____   _____

_____   _____

_____   _____

_____   _____

I am praying for…

_____

_____

_____

I am thankful for…

_____

_____

_____

"There is no problem, I tell you, no matter how difficult it is, that we cannot resolve by the prayer of the Holy Rosary."
Sr. Lucia of Fátima

Sunday, May 10
Mother's Day

Monday, May 11

Tuesday, May 12

Wednesday, May 13
Our Lady of Fátima

Thursday, May 14
St. Matthias, Apostle

Friday, May 15

Saturday, May 16

May 17-23, 2020

To-Do List:

_____   _____

_____   _____

_____   _____

_____   _____

_____   _____

_____   _____

I am praying for…

_____

_____

_____

I am thankful for…

_____

_____

_____

"Love ought to consist of deeds more than of words."

Saint Ignatius of Loyola

Sunday, May 17

Monday, May 18
Pope St. John I

Tuesday, May 19

Wednesday, May 20
St. Bernardine of Siena

Thursday, May 21
The Ascension of the Lord (Holy Day of Obligation, transferred to the following Sunday in many dioceses)

Friday, May 22
St. Rita of Cascia

Saturday, May 23

May 24 – May 30, 2020

To-Do List:

_____   _____

_____   _____

_____   _____

_____   _____

_____   _____

_____   _____

I am praying for…

_____

_____

_____

I am thankful for…

_____

_____

_____

"We know that in everything God works for good with those who love him, who are called according to his purpose."
Romans 8:28

Sunday, May 24

Monday, May 25
Memorial Day (observed)

Tuesday, May 26
St. Philip Neri

Wednesday, May 27

Thursday, May 28

Friday, May 29
Pope St. Paul VI

Saturday, May 30

The Month of
the Sacred Heart
of Jesus

JUNE 2020

Sun.	Mon.	Tues.	Wed.	Thurs.	Fri.	Sat.
	1	2	3	4	5	6
7	8	9	10	11	12	13
14	15	16	17	18	19	20
21	22	23	24	25	26	27
28	29	30				

May 31 - June 6, 2020

To-Do List:

_____   _____
_____   _____
_____   _____
_____   _____
_____   _____
_____   _____

I am praying for…

_____
_____
_____

I am thankful for…

_____
_____
_____

"Do you not know that you are God's temple
and that God's Spirit dwells in you?"
1 Corinthians 3:16

Sunday, May 31
Pentecost Sunday

Monday, June 1
The Blessed Virgin Mary, Mother of the Church

Tuesday, June 2

Wednesday, June 3

Thursday, June 4

Friday, June 5
First Friday, St. Boniface

Saturday, June 6
First Saturday

June 7-13, 2020

To-Do List:

_____   _____
_____   _____
_____   _____
_____   _____
_____   _____
_____   _____

I am praying for…

_____
_____
_____

I am thankful for…

_____
_____

"Life with Christ is a wonderful adventure."
Saint John Paul II

Sunday, June 7
The Most Holy Trinity

Monday, June 8

Tuesday, June 9

Wednesday, June 10

Thursday, June 11
St. Barnabas, Apostle

Friday, June 12

Saturday, June 13
St. Anthony of Padua

June 14-20, 2020

To-Do List:

_____   _____

_____   _____

_____   _____

_____   _____

_____   _____

_____   _____

I am praying for…

_____

_____

_____

I am thankful for…

_____

_____

_____

*"Maintain a spirit of peace and you will save
a thousand souls."*
Saint Seraphim of Sarov

Sunday, June 11
Corpus Christi

Monday, June 15

Tuesday, June 16

Wednesday, June 17

Thursday, June 18

Friday, June 19
The Most Sacred Heart of Jesus

Saturday, June 20
The Immaculate Heart of the Blessed Virgin Mary

June 21-27, 2020

To-Do List:

_____   _____

_____   _____

_____   _____

_____   _____

_____   _____

_____   _____

I am praying for…	I am thankful for…
_____	_____
_____	_____
_____	_____

"Every Christian must be a living book in which others can read the teaching of the Gospel."
St. Joseph of Leonissa

Sunday, June 21
Father's Day

Monday, June 22
Sts. John Fisher and Thomas More

Tuesday, June 23

Wednesday, June 24
The Nativity of St. John the Baptist

Thursday, June 25

Friday, June 26

Saturday, June 27
St. Cyril of Alexandria

The Month of
the Precious Blood
of Jesus

JULY 2020

Sun.	Mon.	Tues.	Wed.	Thurs.	Fri.	Sat.
			1	2	3	4
5	6	7	8	9	10	11
12	13	14	15	16	17	18
19	20	21	22	23	24	25
26	27	28	29	30	31	

June 28 – July 4, 2020

To-Do List:

_____   _____

_____   _____

_____   _____

_____   _____

_____   _____

_____   _____

I am praying for…	I am thankful for…
_____	_____
_____	_____
_____	_____

"For the quality of holiness is shown not by what we say but by what we do in life." - St. Gregory of Nyssa

Sunday, June 28

Monday, June 29
Sts. Peter and Paul

Tuesday, June 30
The First Martyrs of the Holy Roman Church

Wednesday, July 1
St. Junípero Serra

Thursday, July 2

Friday, July 3
First Friday, St. Thomas the Apostle

Saturday, July 4
First Saturday, Independence Day

July 5-11, 2020

To-Do List:

_____   _____

_____   _____

_____   _____

_____   _____

_____   _____

_____   _____

I am praying for…

_____

_____

_____

I am thankful for…

_____

_____

_____

*"He who labors as he prays lifts his heart to God
with his hands." - St. Benedict of Nursia*

Sunday, July 5

Monday, July 6
St. Maria Goretti

Tuesday, July 7

Wednesday, July 8

Thursday, July 9

Friday, July 10

Saturday, July 11
St. Benedict of Nursia

July 12-18, 2020

To-Do List:

_____   _____

_____   _____

_____   _____

_____   _____

_____   _____

_____   _____

I am praying for…

_____

_____

_____

I am thankful for…

_____

_____

_____

"He who desires nothing but God is rich and happy."

St. Alphonsus Liguori

Sunday, July 12

Monday, July 13

Tuesday, July 14
St. Kateri Tekakwitha

Wednesday, July 15
St. Bonaventure

Thursday, July 16
Our Lady of Mt. Carmel

Friday, July 17

Saturday, July 18

July 19-25, 2020

To-Do List:

_____   _____

_____   _____

_____   _____

_____   _____

_____   _____

_____   _____

I am praying for…

_____

_____

_____

I am thankful for…

_____

_____

_____

"The truth is like a lion. You don't have to defend it. Let it loose. It will defend itself." - St. Augustine

Sunday, July 19

Monday, July 20

Tuesday, July 21

Wednesday, July 22
St. Mary Magdalene

Thursday, July 23
St. Bridget

Friday, July 24
St. Sharbel Makhluf

Saturday, July 25
St. James, Apostle

The Month of
the Immaculate Heart
of Mary

AUGUST 2020

Sun.	Mon.	Tues.	Wed.	Thurs.	Fri.	Sat.
						1
2	3	4	5	6	7	8
9	10	11	12	13	14	15
16	17	18	19	20	21	22
23	24	25	26	27	28	29
30	31					

July 26 – August 1, 2020

To-Do List:

_____   _____
_____   _____
_____   _____
_____   _____
_____   _____
_____   _____

I am praying for…

_____
_____
_____

I am thankful for…

_____
_____
_____

"Love is shown more in deeds than in words."
Saint Ignatius of Loyola

Sunday, July 26

Monday, July 27

Tuesday, July 28

Wednesday, July 29
St. Martha

Thursday, July 30
St. Peter Chrysologus

Friday, July 31
St. Ignatius of Loyola

Saturday, August 1
First Saturday, St. Alphonsus Liguori

August 2-8, 2020

To-Do List:

_____   _____

_____   _____

_____   _____

_____   _____

_____   _____

_____   _____

I am praying for…

_____

_____

_____

I am thankful for…

_____

_____

_____

"The Lord is more anxious to forgive our sins than a woman is to carry her baby out of a burning building." – St. John Vianney

Sunday, August 2

Monday, August 3

Tuesday, August 4
St. John Vianney

Wednesday, August 5

Thursday, August 6
The Transfiguration of the Lord

Friday, August 7
First Friday

Saturday, August 8
St. Dominic

August 9-15, 2020

To-Do List:

_____   _____

_____   _____

_____   _____

_____   _____

_____   _____

_____   _____

I am praying for…

_____

_____

_____

I am thankful for…

_____

_____

_____

"Never be afraid of loving the Blessed Virgin too much. You can never love her more than Jesus did."
Saint Maximilian Kolbe

Sunday August 9	
Monday, August 10 St. Lawrence	
Tuesday, August 11 St. Clare	
Wednesday, August 12	
Thursday, August 13	
Friday, August 14 St. Maximilian Kolbe	
Saturday, August 15 The Assumption of the Blessed Virgin Mary (Holy Day of Obligation)	

August 16-22, 2020

To-Do List:

_____   _____

_____   _____

_____   _____

_____   _____

_____   _____

_____   _____

I am praying for…

_____

_____

_____

I am thankful for…

_____

_____

_____

"Make frequent visits to Jesus in the Blessed Sacrament, and the devil will be powerless against you." - St. John Bosco

Sunday, August 16

Monday, August 17

Tuesday, August 18

Wednesday, August 19
St. John Eudes

Thursday, August 20
St. Bernard

Friday, August 21
Pope St. Pius X

Saturday, August 22
The Queenship of the Blessed Virgin Mary

August 23-29, 2020

To-Do List:

_____   _____

_____   _____

_____   _____

_____   _____

_____   _____

_____   _____

I am praying for…

_____

_____

_____

I am thankful for…

_____

_____

_____

"If you believe what you like in the gospels, and reject what you don't like, it is not the gospel you believe, but yourself."

Saint Augustine

Sunday, August 23

Monday, August 24
St. Bartholomew, Apostle

Tuesday, August 25

Wednesday, August 26

Thursday, August 27
St. Monica

Friday, August 28
St. Augustine

Saturday, August 29
The Passion of St. John the Baptist

The Month of
the Seven Sorrows of
the Blessed Virgin
Mary

SEPTEMBER 2020

Sun.	Mon.	Tues.	Wed.	Thurs.	Fri.	Sat.
		1	2	3	4	5
6	7	8	9	10	11	12
13	14	15	16	17	18	19
20	21	22	23	24	25	26
27	28	29	30			

August 30 - September 5, 2020

To-Do List:

_____   _____
_____   _____
_____   _____
_____   _____
_____   _____
_____   _____

I am praying for…

_____
_____
_____

I am thankful for…

_____
_____

"Learn the heart of God from the word of God."

Pope St. Gregory the Great

Sunday, August 30
Monday, August 31
Tuesday, September 1
Wednesday, September 2
Thursday, September 3 Pope St. Gregory the Great
Friday, September 4 First Friday
Saturday, September 5 First Saturday, St. Teresa of Calcutta

September 6-12, 2020

To-Do List:

_____   _____

_____   _____

_____   _____

_____   _____

_____   _____

_____   _____

I am praying for…

_____

_____

_____

I am thankful for…

_____

_____

_____

"Heaven is filled with converted sinners of all kinds,
and there is room for more."
St. Joseph Cafasso

Sunday, September 6

Monday, September 7
Labor Day

Tuesday, September 8
The Nativity of the Blessed Virgin Mary

Wednesday, September 9
St. Peter Claver

Thursday, September 10

Friday, September 11

Saturday, September 12

September 13-19, 2020

To-Do List:

_____   _____
_____   _____
_____   _____
_____   _____
_____   _____
_____   _____

I am praying for…

_____
_____
_____

I am thankful for…

_____
_____
_____

"It is not the finest wood that feeds the fire of Divine love, but the wood of the Cross." – St. Ignatius of Loyola

Sunday, September 13

Monday, September 14
The Exaltation of the Holy Cross

Tuesday, September 15
Our Lady of Sorrows

Wednesday, September 16

Thursday, September 17
St. Robert Bellarmine

Friday, September 18

Saturday, September 19
St. Januarius

September 20-26, 2020

To-Do List:

_____   _____

_____   _____

_____   _____

_____   _____

_____   _____

_____   _____

I am praying for…

_____

_____

_____

I am thankful for…

_____

_____

_____

"The Rosary is the 'weapon' for these times."
Saint Padre Pio

Sunday, September 20

Monday, September 21
St. Matthew, Apostle and Evangelist

Tuesday, September 22

Wednesday, September 23
St. Padre Pio

Thursday, September 24

Friday, September 25

Saturday, September 26
Sts. Cosmas and Damian

The Month of
the Most Holy
Rosary

OCTOBER 2020

Sun.	Mon.	Tues.	Wed.	Thurs.	Fri.	Sat.
				1	2	3
4	5	6	7	8	9	10
11	12	13	14	15	16	17
18	19	20	21	22	23	24
25	26	27	28	29	30	31

September 27 – October 3, 2020

To-Do List:

_____   _____

_____   _____

_____   _____

_____   _____

_____   _____

_____   _____

I am praying for…

_____

_____

_____

I am thankful for…

_____

_____

_____

"Jesus, help me to simplify my life by learning what you want me to be and becoming that person."
Saint Thérèse of Lisieux

Sunday, September 27

Monday, September 28
St. Wenceslaus

Tuesday, September 29
Sts. Michael, Gabriel, and Raphael (the Archangels)

Wednesday, September 30
St. Jerome

Thursday, October 1
St. Thérèse of the Child Jesus

Friday, October 2
First Friday, The Holy Guardian Angels

Saturday, October 3
First Saturday

October 4-10, 2020

To-Do List:

_____ _____

_____ _____

_____ _____

_____ _____

_____ _____

_____ _____

I am praying for…

_____

_____

_____

I am thankful for…

_____

_____

_____

"How beautiful is the family that recites the Rosary every evening." - Saint John Paul II

Sunday, October 4

Monday, October 5
Blessed Francis Xavier Seelos

Tuesday, October 6
St. Bruno

Wednesday, October 7
Our Lady of the Rosary

Thursday, October 8

Friday, October 9

Saturday, October 10

October 11-17, 2020

To-Do List:

_____   _____

_____   _____

_____   _____

_____   _____

_____   _____

_____   _____

I am praying for…

_____

_____

_____

I am thankful for…

_____

_____

_____

"Trust God that you are exactly where you are meant to be." St. Teresa of Avila

Sunday, October 11

Monday, October 12
Columbus Day (observed)

Tuesday, October 13

Wednesday, October 14

Thursday, October 15
St. Teresa of Jesus

Friday, October 16
St. Margaret Mary Alacoque

Saturday, October 17
St. Ignatius of Antioch

October 18-24, 2020

To-Do List:

_____   _____

_____   _____

_____   _____

_____   _____

_____   _____

_____   _____

I am praying for…

_____

_____

_____

I am thankful for…

_____

_____

_____

"Let us throw ourselves into the ocean of His goodness, where every failing will be cancelled and anxiety turned into love." - St. Paul of the Cross

Sunday, October 18
Monday, October 19
Tuesday, October 20 St. Paul of the Cross
Wednesday, October 21
Thursday, October 22 Pope St. John Paul II
Friday, October 23
Saturday, October 24 St. Anthony Mary Claret

October 25-31, 2020

To-Do List:

_____   _____

_____   _____

_____   _____

_____   _____

_____   _____

_____   _____

I am praying for…

_____

_____

_____

I am thankful for…

_____

_____

_____

"Patience is the companion of wisdom."
Saint Augustine

Sunday, October 25

Monday, October 26

Tuesday, October 27

Wednesday, October 28
Sts. Simon and Jude

Thursday, October 29

Friday, October 30

Saturday, October 31

The Month of
the Holy Souls in
Purgatory

NOVEMBER 2020

Sun.	Mon.	Tues.	Wed.	Thurs.	Fri.	Sat.
1	2	3	4	5	6	7
8	9	10	11	12	13	14
15	16	17	18	19	20	21
22	23	24	25	26	27	28
29	30					

November 1-7, 2020

To-Do List:

_____   _____

_____   _____

_____   _____

_____   _____

_____   _____

_____   _____

I am praying for…

_____

_____

_____

I am thankful for…

_____

_____

_____

"Leave sadness to those in the world.
We who work for God should be lighthearted."
St. Leonard of Port Maurice

Sunday, November 1
All Saints' Day

Monday, November 2
All Souls' Day

Tuesday, November 3
St. Martin de Porres

Wednesday, November 4
St. Charles Borromeo

Thursday, November 5

Friday, November 6
First Friday

Saturday, November 7
First Saturday

November 8-14, 2020

To-Do List:

_____   _____

_____   _____

_____   _____

_____   _____

_____   _____

_____   _____

I am praying for…

_____

_____

_____

I am thankful for…

_____

_____

_____

"We must pray without tiring, for the salvation of mankind does not depend upon material success... but on Jesus alone."
Saint Frances Xavier Cabrini

Sunday, November 8

Monday, November 9
The Dedication of the Lateran Basilica

Tuesday, November 10

Wednesday, November 11
St. Martin of Tours, Veterans' Day

Thursday, November 12
St. Josaphat

Friday, November 13
St. Frances Xavier Cabrini

Saturday, November 14

November 15-21, 2020

To-Do List:

_____   _____

_____   _____

_____   _____

_____   _____

_____   _____

I am praying for…

_____

_____

_____

I am thankful for…

_____

_____

_____

"Love begins by taking care of the closest ones –
the ones at home." - Saint Teresa of Calcutta

Sunday, November 15

Monday, November 16
St. Margaret of Scotland and St. Gertrude

Tuesday, November 17
St. Elizabeth of Hungary

Wednesday, November 18
St. Rose Philippine Duchesne

Thursday, November 19

Friday, November 20

Saturday, November 21
The Presentation of the Blessed Virgin Mary

November 22-28, 2020

To-Do List:

_____   _____

_____   _____

_____   _____

_____   _____

_____   _____

_____   _____

I am praying for…

_____

_____

_____

I am thankful for…

_____

_____

_____

"One must see God in everyone."
St. Catherine Labouré

Sunday, November 22
Our Lord Jesus Christ, King of the Universe

Monday, November 23
Blessed Miguel Agustín Pro

Tuesday, November 24
St. Andrew Dũng Lạc and Companions

Wednesday, November 25
St. Catherine of Alexandria

Thursday, November 26
Thanksgiving Day

Friday, November 27

Saturday, November 28
St. Catherine Labouré

The Month of
the Divine Infancy
of Jesus

DECEMBER 2020

Sun.	Mon.	Tues.	Wed.	Thurs.	Fri.	Sat.
		1	2	3	4	5
6	7	8	9	10	11	12
13	14	15	16	17	18	19
20	21	22	23	24	25	26
27	28	29	30	31		

November 29 - December 5, 2020

To-Do List:

_____   _____

_____   _____

_____   _____

_____   _____

_____   _____

_____   _____

I am praying for…

_____

_____

_____

I am thankful for…

_____

_____

_____

"If Mary and Joseph were looking for a home for Jesus, would they choose… your heart, and all it holds?"
St. Teresa of Calcutta

Sunday, November 29
First Sunday of Advent

Monday, November 30
St. Andrew

Tuesday, December 1

Wednesday, December 2

Thursday, December 3
St. Francis Xavier

Friday, December 4
First Friday

Saturday, December 5
First Saturday

December 6-12, 2020

To-Do List:

_____   _____

_____   _____

_____   _____

_____   _____

_____   _____

_____   _____

I am praying for…

_____

_____

_____

I am thankful for…

_____

_____

_____

"Am I not here, I who am your Mother? Are you not under my protection?" - Our Lady of Guadalupe to St. Juan Diego

Sunday, December 6
Second Sunday of Advent

Monday, December 7
St. Ambrose

Tuesday, December 8
The Immaculate Conception of the Blessed Virgin Mary (Holy Day of Obligation)

Wednesday, December 9
St. Juan Diego

Thursday, December 10

Friday, December 11

Saturday, December 12
Our Lady of Guadalupe

December 13-19, 2020

To-Do List:

_____   _____
_____   _____
_____   _____
_____   _____
_____   _____
_____   _____

I am praying for…

_____
_____
_____

I am thankful for…

_____
_____
_____

"A God who became so small could only be mercy and love."
St. Thérèse of Lisieux

Sunday, December 13
Third Sunday of Advent

Monday, December 14
St. John of the Cross

Tuesday, December 15

Wednesday, December 16

Thursday, December 17

Friday, December 18

Saturday, December 19

December 20-26, 2020

To-Do List:

_____   _____

_____   _____

_____   _____

_____   _____

_____   _____

_____   _____

I am praying for…

_____

_____

_____

I am thankful for…

_____

_____

_____

"Mankind is a great, an immense family…. This is proved by what we feel in our hearts at Christmas." - St. John XXIII

Sunday, December 20
Fourth Sunday of Advent

Monday, December 21
St. Peter Canisius

Tuesday, December 22

Wednesday, December 23

Thursday, December 24

Friday, December 25
Christmas Day (Holy Day of Obligation)

Saturday, December 26
St. Stephen

December 27, 2020-January 2, 2021

To-Do List:

_____   _____

_____   _____

_____   _____

_____   _____

_____   _____

_____   _____

I am praying for…

_____

_____

_____

I am thankful for…

_____

_____

_____

"For to us a child is born, to us a son is given... and his name will be called 'Wonderful Counselor, Mighty God, Everlasting Father, Prince of Peace.'" Isaiah 9:6

Sunday, December 27
The Holy Family of Jesus, Mary, and Joseph

Monday, December 28
The Holy Innocents

Tuesday, December 29
St. Thomas Becket

Wednesday, December 30

Thursday, December 31
Pope St. Sylvester I

Friday, January 1, 2021
Solemnity of Mary, the Holy Mother of God (Holy Day of Obligation)
First Friday

Saturday, January 2, 2021
First Saturday

Catholic Prayers

The Prayer by William-Adolphe Bouguereau

The Our Father
Our Father who art in Heaven, hallowed be Thy name; Thy Kingdom come; Thy will be done on earth as it is in Heaven. Give us this day our daily bread; and forgive us our trespasses as we forgive those who trespass against us; and lead us not into temptation, but deliver us from evil. Amen.

The Hail Mary
Hail Mary, full of grace! The Lord is with thee; blessed art thou among women, and blessed is the fruit of thy womb, Jesus. Holy Mary, Mother of God, pray for us sinners, now and at the hour of our death. Amen.

The Glory Be
Glory be to the Father, and to the Son, and to the Holy Spirit. As it was in the beginning, is now, and ever shall be, world without end. Amen.

The Fátima Prayer
O my Jesus, forgive us our sins, save us from the fires of hell, and lead all souls to Heaven, especially those most in need of Thy mercy. Amen.

Grace Before Meals
Bless us, O Lord, and these Thy gifts, which we are about to receive from Thy bounty, through Christ our Lord. Amen.

Grace After Meals
We give Thee thanks for all your benefits, O Almighty God, Who lives and reigns forever; and may the souls of the faithful departed, through the mercy of God, rest in peace. Amen.

Hail, Holy Queen

Hail, holy Queen, mother of mercy, our life, our sweetness, and our hope. To thee do we cry, poor banished children of Eve. To thee do we send up our sighs mourning and weeping in this valley of tears. Turn then, most gracious advocate, thine eyes of mercy toward us, and after this our exile show us the blessed fruit of thy womb, Jesus.

O clement, O loving, O sweet Virgin Mary.

Pray for us, O Holy Mother of God.

That we may be made worthy of the promises of Christ.

The Divine Praises

Blessed be God.
Blessed be His Holy Name.
Blessed be Jesus Christ, true God and true Man.
Blessed be the Name of Jesus.
Blessed be His most Sacred Heart.
Blessed be His most Precious Blood.
Blessed be Jesus in the most Holy Sacrament of the Altar.
Blessed be the Holy Spirit, the Paraclete.
Blessed be the great Mother of God, Mary most holy.
Blessed be her holy and Immaculate Conception.
Blessed be her glorious Assumption.
Blessed be the name of Mary, Virgin and Mother.
Blessed be St. Joseph, her most chaste spouse.
Blessed be God in His angels and in His saints.

The Morning Offering

O Jesus, through the Immaculate Heart of Mary, I offer You my prayers, works, joys and sufferings of this day for all the intentions of Your Sacred Heart, in union with the Holy Sacrifice of the Mass throughout the world, in reparation for my sins, for the intentions of all my relatives and friends, and in particular for the intentions of the Holy Father. Amen.

Memorare

Remember, O most gracious Virgin Mary, that never was it known that anyone who fled to thy protection, implored thy help, or sought thine intercession was left unaided.

Inspired by this confidence, I fly unto thee, O Virgin of virgins, my mother; to thee do I come, before thee I stand, sinful and sorrowful. O Mother of the Word Incarnate, despise not my petitions, but in thy mercy hear and answer me. Amen.

The Act of Contrition

O my God, I am heartily sorry for having offended Thee, and I detest all my sins, because I dread the loss of Heaven and the pains of Hell; but most of all because they offend Thee, my God, Who art all good and deserving of all my love. I firmly resolve, with the help of Thy grace, to confess my sins, to do penance and to amend my life. Amen.

Prayer to Saint Michael the Archangel
Saint Michael the Archangel, defend us in battle. Be our defense against the wickedness and snares of the devil. May God rebuke him, we humbly pray, and do thou, O Prince of the Heavenly hosts, by the power of God, thrust into hell Satan, and all the evil spirits, who prowl about the world seeking the ruin of souls. Amen.

The Creed
I believe in God, the Father Almighty, Creator of Heaven and earth, and in Jesus Christ, His only Son, Our Lord. He was conceived by the Holy Spirit, and born of the Virgin Mary. He suffered under Pontius Pilate, was crucified, died and was buried. He descended into hell. On the third day He rose again. He ascended into Heaven, and is seated at the right hand of God the Father Almighty. He will come again to judge the living and the dead.

I believe in the Holy Spirit, the Holy Catholic Church, the communion of saints, the forgiveness of sins, the resurrection of the body, and life everlasting. Amen.

The Guardian Angel Prayer
Angel of God, my guardian dear, to whom God's love commits me here, ever this day be at my side to light and guard, to rule and guide. Amen.

The Holy Rosary

1. Make the Sign of the Cross and say, "In the name of the Father, and of the Son, and of the Holy Spirit. Amen."

2. Say the Creed.

3. Say one Our Father, three Hail Marys, and one Glory Be.

4. Announce the first Mystery (look on the next page for the Mysteries). Then pray one Our Father, ten Hail Marys, one Glory Be, and one Fátima Prayer while meditating on the Mystery.

5. Then pray one Our Father, ten Hail Marys, one Glory Be, and one Fátima Prayer for each Mystery.

6. After you have completed all the decades, say the Hail, Holy Queen.

7. Make the Sign of the Cross and say, "In the Name of the Father, and of the Son, and of the Holy Spirit. Amen."

The Mysteries of the Holy Rosary

The Joyful Mysteries (Mondays and Saturdays; Sundays during Advent and Christmas):

1. The Annunciation
2. The Visitation
3. The Nativity
4. The Presentation
5. The Finding of Jesus in the Temple

The Luminous Mysteries (Thursdays):

1. Baptism in the Jordan
2. The Wedding at Cana
3. Proclamation of the Kingdom
4. The Transfiguration
5. Institution of the Eucharist

The Sorrowful Mysteries (Tuesdays and Fridays; Sundays during Lent):

1. Agony in the Garden
2. Scourging at the Pillar
3. Crowning with Thorns
4. Carrying of the Cross
5. The Crucifixion

The Glorious Mysteries (Wednesdays and Sundays):

1. The Resurrection
2. The Ascension
3. Descent of the Holy Spirit
4. The Assumption
5. Coronation of the Blessed Virgin Mary

Quotes about the Holy Rosary

"The Rosary is a powerful weapon to put the demons to flight and to keep oneself from sin…. If you desire peace in your hearts, in your homes, and in your country, assemble
each evening to recite the Rosary. Let not even one day pass without saying it, no matter how burdened you may be with many cares and labors."
– Pope Pius XI

"How beautiful is the family that recites the Rosary every evening." - Saint John Paul II

"Among all the devotions approved by the Church none has been so favored by so many miracles as the devotion of the Most Holy Rosary."
– Blessed Pius IX

"You always leave the Rosary for later, and you end up not saying it at all because you are sleepy. If there is no other time, say it in the street without letting anybody notice it.
It will, moreover, help you to have presence of God."
– Saint Josemaría Escrivá

"The Rosary is the 'weapon' for these times."
– Saint Padre Pio

"When people love and recite the Rosary, they find it makes them better."
– Saint Anthony Mary Claret

"Say the Rosary every day to obtain world peace."
– Our Lady of Fátima

"There is no problem, I tell you, no matter how difficult it is, that we cannot solve by the prayer of the Holy Rosary."
– Sister Lúcia de Jesus Rosa dos Santos (seer of Fátima)

"If you say the Rosary faithfully until death, I do assure you that, in spite of the gravity of your sins, you shall receive a never-fading crown of glory. Even if you are on the brink of damnation… sooner or later you will be converted and will amend your life and will save your soul, if – and mark well what I say – if you say the Holy Rosary devoutly every day until death for the purpose of knowing the truth and obtaining contrition and pardon for your sins."
– Saint Louis de Montfort

"[The Rosary] is one of the greatest secrets to have come down from Heaven."
– Saint Louis de Montfort

"The Rosary can bring families through all dangers and evils."
– Servant of God Patrick Peyton

The 12 Promises of
the Sacred Heart of Jesus

We can practice devotion to the Sacred Heart of Jesus by displaying His Sacred Heart prominently in our homes, having our houses Consecrated to the Sacred Heart, and by making the Nine First Fridays in honor of Jesus' Sacred Heart. The following are the promises that Jesus gave to Saint Margaret Mary Alacoque for those who are devoted to His Sacred Heart:

1. I will give them all the graces necessary in their state of life.

2. I will give peace in their families and will unite families that are divided.

3. I will console them in all their troubles.

4. I will be their refuge during life and above all in death.

5. I will bestow the blessings of Heaven on all their enterprises.

6. Sinners shall find in my Heart the source and infinite ocean of mercy.

7. Tepid souls shall become fervent.

8. Fervent souls shall rise quickly to great perfection.

9. I will bless those places wherein the image of My Heart shall be exposed and honored and will imprint My love on the hearts of those who would wear this image on their person. I will also destroy in them all disordered movements.

10. I will give to priests who are animated by a tender devotion to my Divine Heart the gift of touching the most hardened hearts.

11. Those who promote this devotion shall have their names written in my Heart, never to be effaced.

12. I promise you in the excessive mercy of my Heart that my all-powerful love will grant to all those who communicate on the First Friday in nine consecutive months, the grace of final penitence: they will not die in my disgrace, nor without receiving their Sacraments. My Divine Heart shall be their safe refuge in this last moment.

The Divine Mercy Chaplet

Step 1 – Using a Rosary, begin at the cross by making the Sign of the Cross.

(Optional Opening Prayer)
You expired, Jesus, but the source of life gushed forth for souls, and the ocean of mercy opened up for the whole world. O Fount of Life, unfathomable Divine Mercy, envelop the whole world and empty Yourself out upon us.

Step 2 - O Blood and Water, which gushed forth from the Heart of Jesus as a fountain of Mercy for us, I trust in You! (Repeat three times)

Step 3 – On the three beads of the Rosary, pray the Our Father, the Hail Mary and the Apostles' Creed.

Step 4 – Begin each decade with the Our Father beads by praying this prayer:

Eternal Father, I offer You the Body and Blood, Soul and Divinity of Your dearly beloved Son, Our Lord Jesus Christ, in atonement for our sins and those of the whole world.

Step 5 – Complete the decade on the 10 Hail Mary beads by praying this prayer:

For the sake of His Sorrowful Passion, have mercy on us and on the whole world.

Repeat steps 4 and 5 for each decade.

Step 6 – After praying all five decades, pray the following prayer 3 times:

Holy God, Holy Mighty One, Holy Immortal One, have mercy on us and on the whole world.

Step 7 – (Optional Closing Prayer)
Eternal God, in whom mercy is endless and the treasury of compassion inexhaustible, look kindly upon us, and increase Your mercy in us, that in difficult moments, we might not despair nor become despondent, but with great confidence, submit ourselves to Your holy will, which is Love and Mercy itself.

Amen.

The Seven Sorrows Chaplet

According to St. Bridget of Sweden's (1303-1373) visions, the Blessed Virgin promised to grant seven graces to those who meditate daily on her Sorrows:

- "I will grant peace to their families."
- "They will be enlightened about the divine Mysteries."
- "I will console them in their pains and will accompany them in their work."
- "I will give them as much as they ask for as long as it does not oppose the adorable will of my divine Son or the sanctification of their souls."
- "I will defend them in their spiritual battles with the infernal enemy and I will protect them at every instant of their lives."
- "I will visibly help them at the moment of their death-- they will see the face of their mother."
- "I have obtained this grace from my divine Son, that those who propagate this devotion to my tears and dolors will be taken directly from this earthly life to eternal happiness, since all their sins will be forgiven and my Son will be their eternal consolation and joy."

How to Pray the Seven Sorrows (Dolors) Chaplet.

Step 1 – (Optional) Make an Act of Contrition

Step 2 – Pray one Our Father and seven Hail Marys for each of Mary's Sorrows.

> **The First Sorrow:** The Prophecy of Simeon (Luke 2:25-35)
>
> **The Second Sorrow:** The Flight Into Egypt (Matthew 2:13-15)
>
> **The Third Sorrow:** The Child Jesus Lost in the Temple (Luke 2:41-50)
>
> **The Fourth Sorrow:** Mary Meeting Jesus as He Carries the Cross
>
> **The Fifth Sorrow:** Mary at the Foot of the Cross (John 19:25-30)
>
> **The Sixth Sorrow:** Mary receives the Body of Jesus
>
> **The Seventh Sorrow:** Jesus' Burial (Luke 23:50-56)

Step 3 – Pray three Hail Marys in honor of the Blessed Mother's Tears. Pray one Our Father, Hail Mary, and one Glory Be for the Holy Father's intentions. Finally, pray "Virgin Most Sorrowful, Pray for Us" three times.

My Favorite Bible Verses

My Favorite Bible Verses

Regular Prayer Intentions

Regular Prayer Intentions

_____

_____

_____

_____

_____

_____

_____

_____

_____

_____

I am thankful for...

_____

_____

_____

_____

_____

_____

_____

_____

_____

I am thankful for...

Notes

Blessed Candle ends to be buried —

Fr. Keith

#3 Sr. Lisa ✓ ✓ ✓ ✓

Sr. Sylvia

Fr. Raymond

#4 Sr. Susan ✓ ✓ ✓ ✓

Bro. Dez ✓ ✓ ✓ ✓

#3 Sr. Filomena ✓ ✓ ✓ ✓

Br. Alexis

Sr. Sara

Sr. Valeria

Bro. Richard

Notes

— Cendree

— Devins

→ Annette

**Books by Jennifer Harbor Rainey
and Travis Rainey**

A Catholic Prayer Journal for Kids

A Catholic Prayer Journal for Moms

A Catholic Prayer Journal

A Catholic Mom's Guide to Starting a Home Business

The Busy Mom's Meal Planning Journal

My Lenten Journey 2020
(coming early 2020)

If you join my email list, I will send you a free electronic copy of *A Catholic Prayer Journal*. Just send me an email: webmaster@ourcatholiccorner.com. I will not send more than twelve emails each year.
Thank you so much, and may God bless you!

Made in the USA
Monee, IL
08 December 2019